Sunkwa

Sunkwa
Clingings onto Life

Naana Banyiwa Horne

Africa World Press, Inc.

P.O. Box 1892
Trenton, NJ 08607

P.O. Box 48
Asmara, ERITREA

Africa World Press, Inc.

P.O. Box 1892
Trenton, NJ 08607

P.O. Box 48
Asmara, ERITREA

Copyright © 2000 Naana Banyiwa Horne

First Printing 2000

Book design: Krystal Jackson
Cover design: Jonathan Gullery
Cover Art & Illustrations: Amarkai Amarteifio

Library of Congress Cataloging-in-Publication Data

Horne, Naana Banyiwa.
    Sunkwa: clingings onto life / by Naana Banyiwa Horne.
        p.   cm.
    ISBN 0-86543-762-9 (alk. paper). -- ISBN 0-86543-763-7 (pbk.: alk. paper)
    1. Women--Ghana Poetry. 2. Women--Africa Poetry. I. Title.
PR9379.9.H67S86   1999
821--dc21   99-28811
                                                                            CIP

Dedication

To:
My Nananom:
Those in whom my existence is rooted.

Mena Ama Adoma Mensima,
I call on you first.
First face registering my becoming.
It is you who smiled me into this world,
arming me with those lasting lessons in being.

Menana Abba Mbrayeba,
first known to me as Sunkwa,
known to me in spirit but not in flesh.
Without you, Ama Adoma wouldn't be,
and I would never have become.

Meba Araba Sunkwa,
Flesh of my flesh.
Mbrayeba's spirit
rendered flesh in my womb.
Sunkwa,
child of my awakening.
Last to arrive,
first to be chosen.
Sunkwa,
sent to bring me close to my ancestors.

And you others too many to name.
Sage guardians of our sacred founts.
Inductors into the grove of the uninhibited.
Your truth inducing herbs have loosened my
tied tongue, removed the cataracts off my eyes.
Standing in the public arena,
stripped of alienating pride,
I am ready.
Nananom, lead the way!

Sunkwa,
sent to bring me close to my ancestors.

And you others too many to name.
Sage guardians of our sacred founts.
Inductors into the grove of the uninhibited.
Your truth inducing herbs have loosened my
tied tongue, removed the cataracts off my eyes.
Standing in the public arena,
stripped of alienating pride,
I am ready.
Nananom, lead the way!

Contents

Preface

For me, *Sunkwa* has been a process of symbolic self-induced blood-letting that has led to psychic and emotional replenishment. In an immediate, concrete sense, this collection has enabled me to render meaningful that which would otherwise have remained an abnormal storm that blew too fast through the lives of me and my family to leave us enervated in impotence. Nana Araba Sunkwa, my last child, was thrust into our lives on May 21, 1991 and joined the ancestors of the Twidan Abusua of Sentsiwadze, Apaa, and Akwamufie, on June 28, 1991.[1] The writing of *Sunkwa* has become for me the creation of a totem pole to stay me from soul-loss, from insanity; it is my reaffirmation of life over death. Through these poems, my Nana Araba Sunkwa and other people I have encountered who have exited life prematurely can have a stake in immortality.

In its totality, *Sunkwa* is a celebration of life in all its diversity, articulated in five parts. Part One of the collection titled Nananom, commemorates Nana Araba Sunkwa, my mother Adoma, my maternal grandmother, Mbrayeba, also known as Sunkwa, and other people I know—Onisegi, Andrea, and Bigg Redd, among others—who passed on too soon. Part Two, Loves Miracle, explores the intricacies of human relationships. These love poems traverse the erotic to the spiritual. They assert the eternal power of love, affirming human intimacy as the source of our regeneration and sustenance. Part Three, Women Being, speaks to female selfhood and empowerment even as it draws close attention to specific ways in which women's oppression manifest. Part Four, Aborted Becomings, focuses experiences that diminish our selfhood, personal and political; and Part Five, Ancestral Bonds, brings *Sunkwa* full circle, reconnecting with the established norms and totems that inscribe connectedness and transcendence as the key to human redemption.

I am indebted to so many—family and friends, and sisters and brothers of the academy and related professions. Ama Ata Aidoo, 'Molara Ogundipe-Leslie, Mildred Hill-Lubin, Tanure Ojaide, Tuzyline Jita Allan, Obioma Nnaemeka, Janell Agyeman, Diana Embil, Vivian Lee, Wallis and Gene Tinnie,

---

[1]Being from a matrilineage, my child belongs to the matrilineage from which I am descended—the Twidan Abusua/clan of Sentsiwadze, Apaa (Apam) and Akwamufie (Akwamu). It is therefore not a slighting of the father, Adlancy Horne, descended from the Miller family on his maternal side, that his family is not mentioned in this tracing of Sunkwa's lineage.

Raining Deer, and the Miami, Florida global African community—all you who have liked what I have written and encouraged me to write more, I wish to thank you for being unstinting with advise and encouragement and for serving in the capacity of midwives and sympathetic ears. I also wish to thank my brother publisher, Kassahun Checole, and his Africa World Press for making the publishing of *Sunkwa* a reality.

I wish to specially acknowledge Amarkai Amerteifio who has generously exercised his artistic talent to accentuate the message of connectedness, nurturance, transcendence, and the enduring nature of the human spirit that I attempt to articulate through poetic expression. While his talent reveals itself in his artworks, his generosity of heart is evidenced by his taking time out of his busy life to make these illustrations specifically for *Sunkwa*. Without a doubt, the collection, *Sunkwa*, is enriched by his contribution.

Sunkwa, in actuality, belongs to my family natal and marital. John Kofi Amu Nicholson, affectionately referred to by us a Pope John, you who did not merely sire me but fathered and mothered me, you have worked the longest to make me who I am. This work would not have emerged without you. However, the real owners of *Sunkwa* are Adlancy, Kofi Amu Cleotha, Maame Efua Memsima, and Ndyanao Maylena, my husband and children, of whose loss, support, and love of and for Sunkwa I have merely served as a recorder. I can't give enough expression to what you mean to me.

The poems "Madison Revisited" and "Sisterhood" first appeared in *Obsidian II: Black Literature in Review,* and "Damirifa Due" first appeared in *Emerging Perspectives on Flora Nwapa.* "Messages" and "A Note to My Liberal Feminist Sister 1" are appearing in *The New African Poetry: An Anthology*, and "Sounding Drum," "My African Valentine," and "Sore Ka Pra" are appearing in *African Poems of Love.*

—Naana Banyiwa Horne
November 25, 1998

Nananom

Nana Bosompo

I AM
Nana Bosompo.
Genesis of the Waters.
Ever-flowing spirit of Abyssinia.
I AM
Omnipotent Inhabiter
of the Waters of the Guinea Coast.

I AM
Nana Bosompo of old.
Creation flowing through eternity.
Here.
There.
Everywhere.
Endlessly beginning but never ending.

I AM
Nana Bosompo.
Spirit connecting worlds,
differentiating continents.
I AM
deceptive calmness.
Soothing.
Expansively generous.
My waves break e-n-d-l-e-s-s-l-y on countless shores.

I AM
Nana Bosompo.
Eternal fount.
My maternity knows no bounds.
Tuesday is my day.
The world celebrates my fecundity.
My children leave me alone.
On Tuesdays I refurbish the Waters with fish
so the rest of the week, my children can catch fish
or merely frolic, immersed in my maternal warmth.

But I also thunder and rave when I am riled.
Every year I pack mighty Waves and Winds

to avenge my children stolen from Abyssinia.
From the Guinea coast, I hurl hurricanes
against marauders in the Americas.

Every year I moan and I groan,
mourning my children who
remain unburied in watery graves
mapping the Middle Passage.

Every year my grief erupts in
T-E-M-P-E-S-T-S,
reeking havoc on the Americas.
For my maternity knows no bounds.

I AM
Nana Bosompo.
Genesis of the waters.
I AM
Nana Bosompo.
Eternal fount.
Eternally mourning stolen children.

Nananom
(A tribute to those gone on)

Nananom
Hom mbegye nsa nom. . .
Spirit of our Ancestors,
Come partake of this communion. . .

You went away in the company of some giants.
Nana Sunkwa.
My ancestress.
· My child.
Mother of my mother.
My *nana* revisiting.
Now my child, once more departed.
Nana Sunkwa.
This one is for you.
Begye nsa nom.

And you Daughter of Sunkwa.
Ama Adoma Mensima.
Mother of whom I am.
Ye ngya wo ekyir.
How could we not give you your due,
You, who mothered multitudes?
Mena Ama.
I invoke you in all your grandeur.
Adoma ye ntsen bowo ododow.
Wo so begye nsa nom.

Nana Sunkwa, I call on you today,
as I remember these others—
Kubayanda.
Nwoga.
Cartey.
Snyder.
Ferreira.
Bjornson...
Pathfinders saluted as pathmakers.
Nananom of ALA,
and others departed now brought to mind...

Ndyanao.
Onisegi.
Kwamena.
Narcisse...
All you *Nananom* who have gone on,
now together with my Nana Sunkwa.
Hom mbegye nsa nom.

Nana Sunkwa.
You are situated well among giants.
A giant in your own right, Nana,
it is not age but a quality of being—
a potential,
a capacity to inspire,
to unleash,
to tease out,
to tap the hidden potential in others.
This Nana, is what you will always
be remembered for.

Nana, I did not know you.
You whose fate it was to depart
shortly after birthing my mother,
Ama Adoma Mensima.
I did not know you, Nana.
So I invoked you always.
You whose name reminds me to be a seeker,
a seeker of life and all that illuminates my being.
I beseeched you to come to me
in the flesh as you had always been with me
in spirit.

Nana,
I know now you have been here all along,
leading me along paths that keep leading
me to myself.

Kubayanda.
Nwoga.
Cartey.
Snyder.

Ferreira.
Bjornson.
And all you *Nananom* of my awakening.
Ndyanao.
Onisegi.
Kwamena.
Narcisse...
You who are unwillfully omitted,
who have also gone ahead of these;
and you who have gone on since.
All you Ancestral Spirits.
Come partake of this libation.

Mena Ama Adoma Mensima.
Menana Abba Mbrayeba
known to me only in name.
And again Meba Araba Sunkwa,
child of my womb.
Hom nyinaa hom mbegye nsa nom.

Nananom,
Hom mbegye nsa nom.

Sunkwa: A Celebration of Life

Sunkwa,
Steadfast Seeker.
Dauntless Daughter of the Duiker.
Dam the droning drill.

Su wo nkwa.
You who are fated,
to worm in and out of wombs,
bewail your karma.

Su nkwa,
Grandchild of the Talisman-Seeking-Phoenix.
You will find the power within,
to stem the tide of *kwasamba.*

Sunkwa.
Sap of the ancestral home.
You who are to unspell *kwasamba,*
Su nkwa!

Sturdy Mold

Lightly fired clay pot,
how fragile,
oh. . . how frail!

What infirm hands
molded such
ill-placed daintiness?

Life is
a head-on collision,
pitting iron against steel.

Remember! The seasoned tortoise
schooled in eternal patience
serenely plods on.

So keep on
keeping on.
One ant breath by ant breath.

For a Trisomy 13 Child

Child classified *not meant for life,*
where do you find the will
to cling to life?

Fervor defies science and reason
to rendezvous with destiny
in fulfilling life's mission.

As if more keenly aware than all of us
your days are numbered,
you cling to life, savoring every breath.
Drawing from every touch,
from every voice,
from every smile,
you trap life in your palm, folding
little fingers around sturdier fingers.

Existence does not need to occupy
more than a spec in time to be
forever carved into hearts.

The contours of your face.
Your loving pleading eyes.
Your defiantly affirming cry.
Your smile.
The obdurate assertion of your will to prevail
over the frailness of your physical frame.
These and more you have carved forever
into the contours of my own heart.

What matters in life
is not how long
but how fervently we live.

The lesson you came to teach is clear.
Your mission you have unearthed to me
and all who care to see beyond.

Life is precious but fleeting.
Despite that we trap life
through human contact.

The big picture I have gleaned studying you.
And you truly have touched
my life.

It is not the length of our lives,
but how deeply we touch
the lives whose path we cross.

In Memoriam
   (June 28, 1992)

They say time heals all wounds.
So maybe in a decade or a quarter century,
this pain that now is still fresh—like
the open wound in my bikini area,
on the day of your birth—will
acquire the dullness that the caesarian
cut has now acquired.

But right now, though the calendar
tells me it's been a year
since your too-soon-passing,
the wound in my heart bears
the freshness of a brand new cut.

My heart sheds innumerable
tears for the loss of you,
my child.

But tears disappear.
So my will asserts itself in this effort.
I immortalize the memory of you
in words that will contain this pain
pouring out of my heart
this anniversary of your passing ...

I Cried for You Again Today

I cried for you again today,
even though I had not intended to.
But then a siren tore through my heart.
An ambulance careening through traffic,
bearing I know not who, in what
life-threatening condition,
sent gushing to my eyes, tears
I had convinced myself I will no longer
shed for you.

Memories I believed I had buried
under the deepest recesses of my being
usurped my mind.

So I shed another tear
for you
today. . .

Damirifa Due
(for Mamas Selina Kunene and Flora Nwapa)

Damirifa due!
Damirifa due!
Damirifa due!
Due!
Due!
Damirifa Due!

It rained today Mama.
My tears were not enough to fill-up
the rivers to speed you on your journey
to *Samanadze* to join our *Nananom.*
So I called upon the heavens
to open up and weep rain.

The bounty of the heavens, Mama,
matched your bounty to us your children.
The heavens dropped tears in torrents,
washing the skies blue in celebration of
your passing on.

The sun and the rain vied
for your attention today, Mama,
the way your children
often vie for your love.
The sun blazed an eternity,
shining bright and blue,
causing everything to shimmer
in intimation of your mystery.
The sun caused everything to stand
still for your eternity.

The rain fell profusely, steadily,
despite the blazing sun,
filling up the river—the river
to *Nsaman pow mu*—to make
your transit smooth.

Today was a wonder to behold,

Mama, the wonder of you.
You, the sunshine that stayed
our season of frost.

Damirifa due!
Damirifa due!
Damirifa due!
Due!
Due!
Damirifa due!

Song for Onisegi

Onisegi, possessor of precious beads.
I hear you loud and clear.
I hear your joyous call
from the depths of the homestead.

Onisegi, you left so suddenly, we wondered
what wares you brought to the market place
of life that you sold out so fast.

Onisegi, we grieve for you.
We grieve so hard we forget.
You are the favored Daughter of Oya.
Oya, whose winds sweep through the market
faster than stocks change hands
on the New York Stock Market.
And like Oya, you swept through life
like a whirlwind, living life
with such passion.

Onisegi, we realize now
that you tried to prepare us.
To prepare us for the inevitable.
But we were slow to catch on,
seeing only through mortal eyes.
You constantly reminded us there was
so much to learn, so much to do,
so much to pass on to the children,
and so little time to do it ...
And we did not understand.
But now we do, Onisegi.
We understand hard work
never killed any body.
And your going like all goings
was in response to the call of destiny.

But then, one thing bothers me.
And it is your children, Onisegi.
Your children are doing only as well
as orphans do without a mother.
They are still very young.

And like virgin brides on the morning
after, they feel the world's eye on them.
They know the world expects them
to fill your shoes. And Onisegi,
you know yours are some deep shoes
to fill.

Onisegi, your children are coming along.
But they are coming along only as steadily
as toddlers about to take their virgin step.
Their step is frozen because their guide
let go of their hand on the making
of that virgin step.

So Onisegi, don't forget.
Don't forget to do for your children
what only a mother can do for her children.
For even from beyond the homestead,
a mother is still the best to do for her children.

For Andrea

Novinye
I always felt in my heart you would be famous.
And you finally did make the evening news.
You made the local papers too,
breaking the boundaries of anonymity.
But it was neither your beauty,
your ebullience,
your ardor for life,
nor your great intelligence
that was announced to the world.
You did not take the world by storm as a star.
Your undaunted efforts to attain the highest heights
was not what captured the public's eye.

You were first a missing person.
Then you became a slain woman,
stabbed repeatedly to death,
your body locked in the trunk of the BMW
you drove.

Novinye!
You broke our hearts.
You left us numb with disbelief.

     . . .

Novinye
I still have the suitcase.
The things you brought me for my trip
are still in it, registered now in my mind
as the last physical encounter between us
for all time.
I did not get a chance to tell you
I could use neither clothes nor suitcase.
They smelt of smoke.
And I am allergic to smoke,
as you know.

I was going to tell you this
because I was convinced

it would make you
finally quit
smoking.

    . . .

Novinye
I have no forwarding address to which
to send the suitcase.
But you know that is not why I cling to
what was before, a mere object, too flawed
to serve the purpose for which you brought
it to me.
Your suitcase now remains the only
living evidence I have of the fact
that you have been.
So now, Novinye,
I find myself begging your pardon
when I inadvertently knock you down.

    . . .

The bloody red color retains for me
the vibrancy of you.
The Love.
The Life.
The You I know.
I touch the red leather, or is it vinyl?
ever so affectionately,
investing the touch with all
the care,
the love,
I feel for you Novinye.
I have considered sometimes
putting the suitcase in storage
where such articles are stored.
But then we do not lock life away.
Not in closets away from view;
from touch.
So Novinye,
I keep you in the open
where I can see you daily.

    . . .

I have even considered taking
your suitcase to your mother,
or to your next of kin, to whom
it should legitimately be delivered.
But Novinye,
I am not ready to part with you.
Not yet.
. . .

There is so much I wanted to say to you,
I never got around to saying.
So I hang on to your suitcase.
Its red color retaining for me
the vibrancy of you,
sitting in that convenient corner
between my bedroom and bathroom.
. . .

Novinye
I pass you every time.
I pass you in the morning
when I wake up.
And I pass you at night
on my way to bed.
And all the time as I go back and forth,
between bedroom and bathroom,
getting ready to leave home,
or preparing to go to bed,
I hold my daily communion
with you
Novinye. . .

A Dirge for a World Gone Mad

Five little voices happily sing at play.
In the noonday sun, echoes of life
carry over distance, warming lonely hearts.
Five little voices reverberate with life.

Suddenly bullets r-i-c-o-c-h-e-t out of the b-o-o-m-i-n-g
gun of a t-r-i-g-g-e-r-h-a-p-p-y-man.
Five little busy bodies, a breath ago
absorbed in play, lie stilled,
their lives snuffed out to ease the t-w-i-t-c-h-i-n-g
f-i-n-g-e-r-s of a t-r-i-g-g-e-r-h-a-p-p-y- man.

Kindly neighbor dials 911.
Sound of sirens approach in distance.

Five women gather into their arms
the lifeless bodies of five children.
Their little voices warmed hearts
before the b-o-o-m-i-n-g gun
stilled their reverberating voices.

Five women cradle to their hearts
five snuffed out futures.
Other women gather around
five grieving women.
They raise a dirge for their
wasted love and labor.

What a waste!
What a bloody waste!
They wail. . .

The world has gone mad.
The world truly has gone mad.

Bigg Redd

i

Bigg Redd,
we called her.
Bigg Redd she became.
Not because she was bigg,
but she was redd,
redd to the bone.
And she had bigg leggs!
Bigg f-i-n-e strong leggs!

ii

Red skirts were her trade mark:
mini and hip-hugging.
A bigg boodie b-r-o-a-d,
Bigg Redd was f-i-n-e!
Oh, she was so f-i-n-e!

iii

Bigg Redd walked knowing
what she was strutting.
She had a nasty walk,
the nastiest in the hood.
She used to come walking
down the street, kicking it strong.
That's what the men used to say.

iv

Lust would leap right out of men's
eyes and hug Bigg Redd's bigg boodie,
caressing bigg fine leggs.
And Bigg Redd's walk would embrace
manly lust, taking men to incredible highs
to leave them hanging lust-limp.

v

Men looked on Bigg Redd's receding boodie:
Wide open noses sitting expectant,
longing for Bigg Redd's coming.
She had style.
Injected poetry, floating
through a drab world.

vi

Now Bigg Redd is gone.
She's gone! She's gone!
She contracted aids
from the graveyard next door.
She used to go there.
Go for a quick fix.
Until they fixed her up
for good,
too quickly.

vii

The men still talk.
They talk about Bigg Redd.
Talk mixed with some pain
and mostly yearning.
Men miss Bigg Redd's sassy boodie.
Above all, they miss her
nasty walk.

viii

That poem in motion!
BIGG REDD is gone.
She is no more.
She's gone! She's gone!
Bigg Redd is gone
the way many have gone . . .

Love's Miracle

Genesis

Genesis is LOVE.
The Mother of ALL is love.
All-Maker, once happy
alone—not knowing
loneliness—was suddenly smitten.
Filled full-of-love, Creative
Inspiration was born.
And so came the world into
being, born of eternal love.
No longer happy to countenance
aloneness, All-Maker charged
Creation with a mandate:
INCREASE AND MULTIPLY!
Through thick and thin, the world
re-creates itself in love, living
All-Maker's mandate, ensuring eternity.

Armed with this legacy, we stand
Before the world in our turn.
Emboldened by love—the genesis
of our being—we offer ourselves
in total submission
We are not afraid to lose ourselves.
For in submitting, we are
not diminished but fulfilled.
Our once homeless hearts
now find anchor.
Together we take on the world
without fear, armed with twice
the strength of each of us alone.
In love we are doubly enriched.
In place of one family each, we each
have two: two mothers, two fathers,
innumerable siblings, and no end of relatives.
Love is indeed the genesis of our life.
In love, we dare declare, we are.

Sounding Drum

There is a universe buried inside of me.
A hibernating hide
waits
anxiously
to be sounded.
Sounded by the vibration that is you.

The inside of me is a sounding drum.
A pulsating drum,
suspended,
pulsing,
toned,
by the tenderness that is you.

I am a universe.
A drum sounded into life by the rhythm
that is you.
Your heart drums me into sound.
Your heart beats my drum,
my song.

At last!
The drum that is me
vibrates with rhythm
that is you.

Happy Father's Day!
June 20, 1992

I wake up with you on my mind.
Man of my life,
begetter of my children.
I wake up breathing,
tasting,
feeling,
smelling,
seeing you.
Not in my minds eye, but in my being.
Sewn as you are inside the fabric of my being.

So I console myself I can stand
this physical separation imposed
by the necessity of our lives
and all the lives that tie into ours.
I leave you with all I love
and set out, the proverbial heroine.
I go to slay the dragon that dogs our lives.

I come back wiser than I left maybe,
but certainly bearing fruit—the stock
of that harvest we sowed together
at the beginning of our becoming.

On this father's day away from you,
I hail you father-mother-companion.
Progenitor of me and ours,
I cannot find enough ways to serenade you.
Oyeadze!
Me da wo fom.

You Rock My World

You rock my world,
man of primeval passions.
Your rousing touch ignites
every atom in my care ridden body.

Miracle maker
injecting life blood into me,
I cherish your invitations
to the threshing floor of healing.

For always I emerge, purged of all tension,
resonant in rhythms that are vibrantly radiant.
Your manhood draws out my womanhood.
Your touch lifts me high above life's drudgery.

My maker must have given you the key
to my sanctuary.
For you have unlocked the door
to the secret of my life.

Miracle worker
Your touch unleashes
that primal joy of knowing
how well loved I am.

My African Valentine
(To my husband: February 1992)

Your love, pumpkin, is rain
falling, full,
filling my seed time.

Into the snugness of my soil,
you seed, pumpkin, burrowing deep,
sprouting lush evergreens.

Your warm embrace is lusty
pumpkin leaves snugly wrapped
around me.

And your bounty erupts
into myriad *egusi* seeds
perennially in bloom.

Sore Ka Pra: Whoopie, Akan Time.

Before alarm clocks,
Akans had *Sore ka pra.*
Sore ka pra of tender genesis.
Rousing feather strokes, energizing drowsy wives.
Husbands passionately beget happy homemaking.

Sore ka pra!
"Wake up and go sweep" erupts into
husband passions pestling tender
offerings into enraptured mortars.
Wives bask sensuously in
the tender embrace of husbands.
The rhythm of pestles encircled
by the syncopation of mortars.

Sore ka pra!
Cherished secret of women breezing through
their day's chores.
Fully-sated, wives spill marital contentment,
creating anew a slumbering world
in intricately executed broomstrokes.
Signatures!
Signifiers
of marital bliss.

Madison Revisited
(for Mama and Papa Kunene)

Time has a way of conniving with distance
to dull the edges of our rememories.

So distanced from those living presences
insulating me from chilling countenances
the alienating glare of white snow
the anesthetized cut of steel blue eyes

settled raw
threatening

sub-zero winters and frost-bitten memories.

Alienation's pulse is harsh
splintered bones in snowfalls.

But now as I sit so close to you
enveloped again in your warm nearness,
the sharp edges thaw off remembrances
of glowing friendships encircling alienating
white spaces in hot flushes of colored memory.

Nostalgia wells strong within as numbing
edges thaw off.
And once more, I taste
glimmers of sunshine and rainbow arches
traversing frozen snow to bear me over this
paralysis.

Becoming

If I give myself to you,
will you and I become one?
And what kind of union will we become?

If you and I become one,
will we evaporate into nothingness,
into neither you nor I,
leaving behind a vacuum,
emptiness,
spacelessness.

If you and I become one,
will our generations terminate?
Instead of support will you swallow me up?
Choke the very life out of me?
Suck up my breath and leave me no room
to thrive, to bloom, to become?
Will you consume me so there will no longer be me?

They tell me there is not but so much room
for only one of us can grow.
That the survival of the individual of necessity
happens at the expense of others.
That self preservation is the primary
determinant of relationships.
So for you to grow, *I* must of necessity atrophy.
I should not worry my pretty little head
about such unresolvable issues.

But then, I have also looked around me.
And I have seen creatures
who start off in positions of need and strength.
The strong do not grow strong at the expense of the needy.
The strong give freely of strength to the weak.
The weak grow steady in the strength of the strong.
The strong do not grow weak from supporting the needy.

Together they grow.
Become a unite of support,
a family.

So if I give myself to you,
will your strength overshadow me?
Will you demand that I stop being so you can become?
Or will you be strong enough to be
so I can be?

Woman Being

My Fair Lady

My fair lady is no delicate lady.
She is, in fact, no lady at all.
She is an African woman
ripe and mature,
ripened by her heritage of being
a stronger breed among strong breeds.
Gracefully, she bears humanity
on her strong firm back.

My fair lady is an African woman
whose fertility is undisputed.
First birthing herself,
she birthed the first man,
populating the world with her talented offspring.
You encounter her multicolored
descendants all over the globe.

My fair lady is a beautiful African
woman of firm strong breasts.
Her firmness comes from no implants.
Eternal fountain of nurturing,
She stays firm and full
suckling the world.

My fair lady is a copper brown woman
deep with rich tones of one
emerged from earth's womb.

She is the progenitor of the human race.

Woman Being

A woman is not a thing,
a mannikin waiting,
eveready to be pawed
when man's juices are stewed
ready to spurt an explosion
to punctuate a masturbation.

Creator, you are woman.
Life-pulse of all that is human.
Nerve centering the universe.
Essence fused to incense.
Woman you pulsate too much nutriment
to be wasted in non-fulfillment.

A Note to My Liberal Feminist Sister (1)

The issue for me, Sister,
is not whether I have been
knocked up or knocked down,
borne unwanted children from sexual
acts to which I did not give my consent.
It is not to count how many times
a fist has been slammed into my jaw,
an unwanted penis thrust into my vagina.
Befouling eyes devour my body on the job
while I desparately strive to convince I am
the brain that was hired to do the job.
Sister,
I cannot wallow in self-pity or internalize victim status.
Neither do I have the luxury to immortalize
my victimization by making art of my
degradation—playing victim scenes
over and over like a broken needle,
caught in the same groove on the record,
unable to play the entire song out.
Really, Sister!
Do we have time to quibble about whether
I am in denial, repressed, or simply so
frequently abused that I have lost
consciousness of what constitutes abuse?

The real question for me, Sister,
is how I am going to rise from the ground up
after I have been knocked down;
keep a song in the hearts of all my children,
wanted and unwanted.
It is how we are going to manage to stay up
and avoid being dragged back down.
That struggle, Sister, is enough to consume
whatever energies we have left, considering
all the ways invented to keep us down
on the ground.

Emersion

Some days I do not want to emerge
from the womb of sorrow
springing to entomb me.

Silk-spinning cocoon
spins sorrow-threads to enshrine me.
Kente grief drapes tightly around me.

Soul-mate fine-tuned to my life rhythms.
You intercept those soul-sapping vibes
before they enthrone themselves in me.

Then old souls in little bodies
catapult me out of sorrow to enshrine me
in a real world of cares.

They immerse me in matching socks
and clean underwear, marinated
in hugs and kisses.

Sisterhood

Sisterhood reigns supreme in my world.

A world of sisters encircles me,
fanning my ego,
propping me up.
It is to sisters I owe my sassiness,
my special flare,
my style,
my exuberance,
my nerve,
my sense of my specialness.

You wonder how I do dare be so irrepressible?
I dwell in a world filled with an array of sisters (blood and
acquired);
and some brothers are also sisters.
Mine is a gynosphere tinted with colorful laughter.

Sisterhood is what reigns supreme in my world.

But then some brothers are also sisters.
Mothering fathers roll motherhood and fatherhood into one.
Sisterly brothers do not trip sisters,
do not let them fall flat on their faces.
Brothers weave manly strength into
billowy blankets on which sisters repose.

So if I openly confess I am a man-loving woman
turned on by manhood,
made giddy with desire by sweat glistening on manly bodies,
sent whistling by good looks in brothers,
it is because I know some brothers are also sisters.

Should it puzzle you that my world is
enriched by mothering males, admirers of all ages?
Father, husband, brothers (blood and acquired), sons, nephews?
Beautyful bronze blacker-than-blue-brothers
are numbered among my sisters;
for some brothers are also sisters.

Sisterhood indeed reigns supreme in my world.

WAKE UP!!!!!!!!!!

MOTHERS OF THE WORLD,
WHERE HAVE YOU GONE?
WHAT EVIL BEAST ENSNARES YOU?
HOW CAN YOU DOZE
WHEN CARNAGE THREATENS ALL AROUND?

RISE, MOTHERS!
SNAP OUT OF YOUR STUPOR!
RISE UP!
FOR THERE IS NO ONE,
NO ONE BUT YOU
TO RECLAIM OUR LOST WORLD.

It is not in the nature of mothers
to countenance death coolly
and not lift a finger to stem its tide.
So trapped in the midst of the walking-dead,
caught in the throes of a death-dance,
take fate in hand.
Descend on the underworld!
Don't let birth pangs get
trampled under calloused feet.
Don't leave once lively children
to be rendered skeletons—Zombies
from whom all life is sucked.
Our legacy of life should not,
will not, be reduced to a desecrated
tabloid of broken bodies and snapped souls!
Arm yourselves with dug-up umbilical cords.
Make haste and wrap your lappas.
Descend on the underworld
and resurrect your children.

After all, who knows the secret to life
better than those who suffer birth pangs?
WAKE UP!
M-O-T-H-E-R-S!!!!!!!
W-A-K-E U-P!!!!!!!!!!!!!!!!!!!!!!!!!!!!!!!

A Note to My Liberal Feminist Sister (2)

Sister?
I query because I don't believe
you are a sister.
Yes, you are female.
You have tittties and a pussy just like me.
Yes, just like me.
But that is where the resemblance between us stops.

You speak not in the voice of the raped but the rapist.
You definitely do not decry my violation
but glorify the inglorious act of my violator,
milking my degradation in pursuit of fame.
With your offensive art enacting violent
sexual scenes in which you scream in ecstacy,
begging to be fucked, urging your assailant
to ravish you, asserting the rapist's misperception
that women crave nothing better than to be fucked,
that in fact without saying it, we are actually begging
to be fucked every time we step out,
you are endangering the lives of women.

When my assailant forcibly thrust
his venom into my unyielding
spaces—hell-bent on forcing me
to cry out, to assert his dominion over me,
to free him of the burden of his own violence,
his beastiality—I would not urge him on
with ecstatic cries of "Fuck me,
I was born to be fucked!"
In that interminable space with everything
inside me numb except for the shame-faced pain
creeping around the corners of my disembodied self,
I did not, through that whole ordeal,
for once, acquiesce: "Fuck me!"
So if all you can offer me is your "B" rated
enactments of sexual aggression against women
who succumb to the shattering
of the sanctity of their sacred spaces,
then you are no Sister, sister!

Impartial Mother

Moon high up in the sky.
Impartial mother.
Boundless bounty
reaching down indiscriminately
to all your children.
Moon, you mesmerize all
with your quiet radiance.

Awesome beauty.
Appeal without parallel.
Indulgent matriarch with neither
an intimidating nor alienating bone.
Moon, your magnetism draws,
galvanizing all longingly to you.

You are not the sun whose
radiance overpowers,
overwhelms.
Moon, you are seductive
queen in whose sensuousness
humankind shamelessly basks.

A woman unsurpassed.
Mother/lover, Moon.
Your effulgence dusts
us all in magic.

Aborted Becoming

I
Fiery muscle,
pulsing,
radiating.
Ball throbbing,
warm,
anticipating.

Expectancy
lodges firmly
within.

My womb—a
bud about to
blossom.

My heart—radiant,
pulsant,
expectant.

II
A fiery ball of lead
now sits heavy
within.

My heart,
a loadstone, galvanized.
Dead.

Lead trigger,
spitting searing shots,
singe my womb.

III
What was conceived—a
fecund womb,
incubating
neonate—is now
cold.

Sepulchered.
My womb, sans warmth.
A tomb, devoid
of light.

Ain't Life a Bitch?

The expression life is a bitch
assumes terrifying clarity
on days like these.

Car break downs.
Plumbing malfunctions.
First day of school for kids.
Deadlines on bills
paid to endless ends.
And car-
      less
           worlds.

What goes by?

Designated jobs have moved
to remote planets
whose remote controls
have migrated to obscure corners.

Set alarm clocks
do not bring wakefulness
ringing out long departed
notes from care-
          free
            worlds
filled with ease
         full
of
     bliss.
They transport tired souls
to a land of dreams
where there are
no mean bill collectors.
Definitely no slave-driving bosses.
Only sweet harmonizing
music swinging me
           low
out of earthly
       woes.

Swing me low,

Sweet chariot.
Come and carry
me out of this shrill trill
bordering the edges
of my dream of ease
                    full
of
        bliss.

In my world of slumber, I hear
the trumpet of the heavenly jazz band,
headed by no others than *Sachimo* and *Dizzy*,
swinging me
                low
                        on horns
                                on high
                                        to ecstasy.

Threatening, piercing ring shatters
the serenity of my dream world.
My waking world now hangs
on the thread of a telephone line.
Shrill voice of angry social workers query:
Why are children not in school
this first day of school?

Over-burdened mothers have
no chance to dream up convincing excuses.
No thanks to MA BELL and her conveniences.
Not-so-polite-voices intrude in waking lives,
shattering all dreams of solitude.

Why have you not honored your promise to make
good on a payment at the down-town office?
                    Remember?
You called begging for a reasonable payment plan.
You promised to make this payment good.
Your bill is already past due.
You are risking a good credit rating!

                    .   .   .

Mortal wounds are constantly dealt
to the pride of over-indulging mothers

with demanding children who always
want
        and want
           and want
in megadoses that dwarf all sense of creditability.

In the land of the brave and the free,
only the hardened are truly free.
They wheel and deal.
They make or break.
They mortgage us whose
entrails are delicately
marinated in morality sauces.

The telephone is not a life-line for the underdog.
Not for mothers who are workers,
dependent on the goodwill or lack thereof
of slave-driving bosses and temperamental babysitters.

Answering machines impersonate
disembodied voices of care-givers
when they are most desperately
needed by working mothers
saddled with inclement work schedules
drawn up by supervisors whose lives are
neatly packaged in designer clothes
impervious to the pleading eyes
of needy children.

The ring of the telephone always spells
doom for over-burdened mothers with demanding
bosses and half-hearted child-care-givers.

*Sorry-but-I-cannot-keep-your-babies-today-
I-have-an-engagement-which-conflicts-with-the-time-
you-expect-me-to-watch-your-babies.*

*You are fired!
With profits dwindling and unseasonable
demands for raises,
I cannot afford to keep slack old you!*

      . . .

Life is a bitch.
I cannot cope.
I'm totally stunned
out of my wits.
Lord how I crave
to be free from care.
Why have I . . .
Don't even think it!

These wakeful children.
They will not leave me be.
They come climbing.
All over me
                    they roll
                              they laugh
                                        they tickle.
They bring to a life almost lost
a new lease!

Wonhyia o! Black Women Beware!
(For Ma Brookes)

My foremother's hair was singed
from a potable hell she bore.
On black foremother's head sat a containable inferno
designed for the head of widowed black women.

Singed black hair.
Insignia of fallen black womanhood.
Singed black hair.
Blazing crowns of widowed womanhood.

My dreading widowed foremother wore
a coiffure of glowing coals in iron pot.
Her blazing coiffure branded into her head
her condition of hell as a woman without a man.

Life, she is instructed, is a veritable hell
for a woman without her man,
her lord,
Divine guardian of her loins.

What is a woman to do
with no man to lord it over her?
Lord,
what is a woman to do?

Widowed foremothers bore burning
infernos of glowing coals on their heads.
They embarked on their pilgrimage into widowhood,
trailing the smell of singeing hair through the air.

ii
Wonhyia o! Wonhyia o! Wonhyia o!
All women beware!
Widowed woman's warning cry
careens through the air.

Wonhyia o!
Daughters open your eyes.

Widowed foremother warns.
Open your eyes to the fate of widowed womanhood.

Wonhyia o!
Wives beware of reckless men!
Beware of outliving
too-soon-dead men.

Wonhyia o!
Hard-loving women, beware!
Beware of being branded Black widow spiders
who send men to early graves.

iii
Beautyful, healthy black hair
marks proud black womanhood.
Singed, deceased hair blazes
fate of black widowhood.

Widowed foremothers bore burning
infernos of charcoal pot on their heads
en route to the sea to be purified
of the stench of contaminating death.

At their destination their heads were shorn
to make room for virgin hair to sprout.
But the smell of singed black hair prevails.
Branded memory of widowhood prevails.

iv
Wonhyia o!
The scream of black foremothers
reach out to us in warning.
Beware black women of the stench of singed hair.

Y'ehyia o!
Fate has overtaken us!
Fate indeed has overtaken us.
The warnings of black foremothers have gone unheeded.

Y'ehyia o!
Now black women willingly wear
the insignia of black widowhood.
Black women singe beautyful, healthy, black hair.

Y'ehyia o!
Y'ehyia o!!
Y'ehyia o!!!

What is in a name?

Mary, Maria, Mariamma.
Name riffled with contrarieties.
Mary of all women you alone have
unlocked the cult of *True Womanhood*.
You are hailed, Virgin!
Upheld to be emulated by all women.

Mary, celebrated Mother of God.
Alone you have accomplished that
of which every woman only dreams:
Womanhood attained without
succumbing to sexual conquest.
Is it any wonder you are the envy of all women?
You, who conceived a child out of wedlock
and earned a husband and the crown of Virgin.
You gain in stature where
other women are diminished.
Hailed the world over, You are
The Blessed One Amongst All Women.

What is your secret? Mary.
Other women following your footsteps
fall from grace.
They bear bastard children and forfeit
any claim to *True Womanhood*.
But your unfathered child is no bastard.
He is proclaimed God's
Only Son among mortals!

Mary, You are powerful indeed!
Hail! Mary.
Hail! Virgin/Whore!

Who Am I?

I am no Job
suckled on woe's tit
to be bound in allegiance
to a god cloaked in vengeance.

I am a *Fantse* woman
sculptured from love
repulsed by a brute maker
as I am by a brute lover.

I know not Job's mother.
I know not Job's father.
I am no kin to Job.
I understand not Job's sob.

Job and I speak no common language.
We share no common heritage.
He is a freak hooked on pain.
And I thrive on sunshine and rain.

Figurines

I am not
I'm not
am not
creasing my forehead
because I am deep in thought
figuring how to invest my millions
so I can reap billions.

I am not figuring on how
to capitalize on human misery.
To find a sorely raped country
freshly bleeding, tottering
on the brink of annihilation
so I can camouflage human exploitation
as divine intervention.

My forehead is creased because
I am deep in thought figuring how
to stretch an emaciated paycheck
disbursed before deposited
over 30 or 31 long days
and sleepless nights.

Days filled with arduous work
talking from sunup to sundown
filling still impressionable minds
with stretched-truths that do not
add up to balance meals,
pay up utilities,
rent,
clothing,
transportation,
a movie every now and then,
save towards the children's education,
adequate health and dental care...

I am not
even about keeping up with the
Joneses.

I am figuring how to balance
a staple of beans and antacids
with fish once a week.
More soup,
fruit,
salad,
assorted vegies,
juice rather than cheap soda.
A steak maybe twice a month.
And don't give me no crap
about red meat and it not
being good for my health.
I haven't eaten enough of it
to even start to remember
what it tastes like.

What definitely needs eliminating
is the staple of antacids needed to
contain too many bean diets.

I am figuring on how long
the landlord's tolerance will endure.
How to extricate myself from the vicious
circle of fines for overdue bills.

I am figuring on when some savior
will invent an elastic paycheck—a
paycheck that will stretch
to accommodate 28, 29, 30 or 31
days to a month,
as father time deems fit
to stretch time.

Messages

Anyemiyo.
Do you remember *Oshimashi?*
In our heyday
the prospect of spending
even a little time with him
we considered so preposterous
the thought of it would send us
giggling.
And then we would fittingly
punctuate our contempt with
a hiss,
hissing
as only highly affronted Ghanaian females
could hiss.

Rokpokpo.
That was our nickname for him.
Remember?
Rokpokpo.
A name inspired by the mere
look of his clothes which were
in cahoots with some invisible
force to obey the wind.

Of course,
knowledge of the man inside
the clothes made evident
we could not have chosen
a more fitting name for him.
He definitely was as flaky as
his *rokpokpo* clothes.

Ei *Anyemiyo.*
Now I hear *Oshimashi*
with his *rokpokpo* self
is an officer of state.
The wind has blown him
right into the lap of opportunity.
His *rokpokpo* clothes are now
gone with the wind.

He sports three piece suits
custom-made in Paris and Rome.
His ashen blotchy skin has followed suit.
He looks like a candidate for
a skin tone cream commercial.
When he is not jetsetting and hobnobbing
with our former slavers,
he is lulling around in a plushly
carpeted air-conditioned office
in that castle by the sea.

Anyemiyo.
I hear *Oshimashi Rokpokpo*
has sworn vengeance
on all those who did not see worth
when it was shrouded in *rokpokpo* clothes.
He sent a friend to warn us.
He wants us to know
it is not too late for us
to make his special guests list.

Of course,
you know how I answered his messenger.
First I giggled.
Just like the old days.
And then I hissed.
I hissed long and sensuous.
I hissed,
as only a mature Ghanaian woman,
who doesn't give a damn about the
Rokpokpos of the world, can
hiss.

Aborted Becomings

Alienation Blues

What did I do to be so black and blue?

Seduced.
I am now severed
from the force that defines my center.
Unclaimed.
Untouched.
Alone.
I have become an island
Inundated by expanses of water.
Other lands are visible.
Yet none plays touch with me.
When I reach out desperate for contact,
all I reach is water.
Damming waters defining my isolation.

What did I do to be so black and blue?

Elusion
(for Dominic, and all those students who eluded me)

At last your face emerges,
riddling my mind's eye.
Questions bounce off cerebral walls
screeching, but not seeking answers.

Is it already too late to rake
the coals to ignite a mind atrophied?
Complacency negotiates, breaking no boundaries.
Is it much easier to let slip out of reach?

High Tech Love

Good old fashioned courting
has become yet another
casualty.

In this high tech age,
it is absolutely uncool
for man to walk up to woman
make friendly conversation
express a desire to visit
or waste time getting to know
her.

And whatever you do,
absolutely do not,
do not fall in love.

When you need some loving,
by all means do reach out.
Do not reach out to touch
someone.
Reach for your cellular phone
and
dial 1-900 MASTURBATE.
Eroticized help will
reach you
wireless.
So you can touch
yourself.

Camp David, the Crack House in the Hood

The new world inferno is a gilded tomb,
a graveyard sitting right next door to you.
It is Camp david, that crack house in the hood,
which mocks the coveted retreat of the elect.
It tops all obscene jokes, peddling quick
fixes for the malaise of the masses.

Camp david is a hovel for pushers,
peddlers of death capsuled in white.
It beckons people from far and near,
beaming ignited rocks, puffing out
false hope from apocalyptic pipes.

Desperate acolytes eager for a quick fix
flock nightly to exuberate at camp david.
Come the morning, they emerge—
zombied-gaping-ravenous-eyeless-sockets.
They are stoned by little white rocks into
gilded tombs.

Look at that Zombie

Look at that zombie.
Yes!
Look at her stumbling through
the alleys and byways of life,
scavenging for crack.
Nothing else exists for her now except crack.
Yes!
Take a look at her.

Look at her once beautiful eyes
now gaping lifeless sockets staring sightlessly
out on the world she has fallen out of.
Tarnished skin stretches taut over
what used to be a lively face,
now frozen into an eternal grimace.

If you dare look closely at that zombie,
you might recognize the ghost of
the beautiful girl you went to school with.
She was a hot number then.
All the boys including the ones you would
have liked to date flocked around her,
drooling over her every move.
She had fine legs then, and she
had a chest and a butt to boot.
She had a figure that declared her
a woman even then, when you were still
an undifferentiated mass of asexual flesh.

She was the one who broke the heart
of that boy you would willingly have laid
down for if only he would notice you.
She was the nightmare of your adolescent life.
She had then everything your eager heart
craved from life—beauty/friends/popularity/
self-assuredness/notoriety—and she could
dance, the crown of all parties.

But now you look at that zombie!
Look at that nightmare of your adolescent life
now become the nightmare of the world.
She is dead to everything but crack.
A cockroach crouching in dark alleys.
Her eyeless sockets gape lifelessly
out on a world she has fallen out of. . .

What Used to Be Our Play Song

Mami Mami ke mi tolo
Mami Mami ke mi tolo

That was our play song.
We grew up singing it,
loosing the self to the license
of crowding the mother of choice.
The one condoning enough
to encourage our playful abandon
by dispensing *pesewas* and other little
tokens of maternal recognition
to grace our performance.

Mami Mami ke mi tolo
Mami Mami ke mi tolo

We loved to raise our voices in song,
for the song to rap our bodies
in the spirit of rhythm.
A rhythm fueled by the security
of being numerous children
with innumerable mothers.
Mothers eager to shower
love to safeguard self-worth.

Mami Mami ke mi tolo
Mami Mami ke mi tolo

A ritual of children playfully
begging for pennies and crumbs
of maternal indulgence informed
by the sheer joy of knowing that
the circle of assured love
will never be broken.
This ritual enactment of children's
need for maternal rewards
seals a mutual interdependence.

Mami Mami ke mi tolo
Mami Mami ke mi tolo

71

That was our play song.
We sang it long ago
in another life time,
in a different world,
a world ringed by sacred
bonds secure and unshakable.

And now I hear the same song,
our love song sang by strangers
in broken chords reverberating
with the menace of desperation.
The singers no longer beg
in jest but in earnest.
They are no playful children
forming an unbroken circle
around doting mothers whose
happiness seals our security.

They are grown men and women,
and occasionally children,
singing what used to be our song
in discordant notes.
It is sung at interceptions.
It is sung at traffic lights.
It is sung on side walks.
It is sung from storefronts.
It is mumbled everywhere
givers can be accosted.

These new singers of my song
are beggars in ernest.
Their singing comes muffled,
the ring of joy and laughter
present when we solicited
attention from indulgent mothers
replaced by the dullness of menace
and fear marinated in desperation.

The beggar doesn't want to beg
any more than the giver coerced
into giving by shame wants to give.
For giving now affirms
the entrenchment of a crime
scarring both giver and taker.

The spared know without looking
when shame-faced beggars
emboldened by want approach.
So before they can break into
their discordant song, the spared
hasten to buy their conscience
for however much comes
quickly to hand.
A dollar.
A five.
A ten.
Even a quarter.
A transaction conducted
without acknowledgement.

Unobtrusively givers hasten to give,
acting to stay their minds from conceding:
There but for the grace of God,
measured one or two paychecks
away go I.

Life in Retreat

When life retreats from center stage,
refusing the seat of honor,
life slouches on the stoop of the courtyard,
skirting the peripheries of existence.

The jousts, the tussles, the tumbles,
consuming the potent drift dull,
lacking luster for life in retreat.

The endless mind-games of the introverted
has as much allure for life in retreat
as the feeble flicker of love grown overly familiar.

Life in retreat is a lukewarm lover.
Before him sensuality fizzles flat,
overexposed champagne bereft of bubbles.

Those who remember life at center-stage
wonder what evil cat got life's tongue.
They wonder what ferocious feline
felled life and disembowelled it of zest.

Stark Reality
(a parable)

Why does love after "I do" wane?
When battle is won doesn't
the desire to quell the enemy fade?

When the hunter who starts the hunt,
one among a pack of hounds,
at last corners the game,
his fellow hunters acknowledge his claim
to the spoil of the hunt
and fall back in deference
to his claim.

Fellow hunters,
now losers, envy Victor's trophy.
They enshrine Victor in awe.
They marvel at his valor
and covet *the prize*
now mounted on a pedestal
to command public adulation.

But the hunter
no longer inspired to hound, retires.
Victor retires to bask in ease,
the desire for action
departed with the possession
of *the prize.*

When battle is won
is there any more need for
Victor to prove his valor?

Gbevu

Gbevu!
The body you planted
has sprouted.
It has sprouted.

Gbevu!
The corpse you planted
in the trunk of that BMW
has sprouted.

Gbevu!
You should have known
it would sprout.
You should have known.
After all, when we plant seeds
don't they sprout
to announce to the world
the fruits of our labor?

Gbevu!
Your decomposing corpse
has sprouted.
The stench
from the body you planted
has reached the nostrils
of the world.

Gbevu!
The devious seeds you sowed
under the blanket of night
have now sprouted.
Your devious seeds
have sprouted
with the quickness of seeds
dropped in the bottomless
muck of the everglades.
Gbevu!

Gbee Baa Wa Oyi!

They said it.
Yes, they said it.
The Ga people said:
Dogs will bark at you.
And we are all witnesses.
Dogs are barking at you.
Dogs are barking it out
for the whole world to hear.
Dogs are barking out
how you came to be
the big shot we all kiss up to.

Remember that jive saying:
Dogs will bark at you?
Yes, we used to say it.
Dogs will bark at you.
When we were growing up in Accra.
Dogs were barking everywhere you turned.
We thought then it was a joke.
But joke or not
dogs are barking at you.

Dogs are barking out
your misuse of power,
the political power invested in you
by people you have betrayed
by your corruption.

Dogs are barking out
your appropriation of the funds
collected for the development
of the community that voted
you into power.
Dogs are barking about
those monies you diverted
into Swiss bank accounts
for your large-living.
Dogs are barking these things out
for the whole world to hear.

Dogs are barking at us.
Dogs are barking at us because
they can smell the stink of corruption
the rest of us fail to smell for convenience.
We have been too busy fishing
crumbs from your over-laden table
to expose your wrong-doing.

Dogs are barking at you.
Dogs are barking at us.
Dogs are barking.
Dogs are barking.
Barking...
Barking...

Flint and Bolts

Flesh and flint!
Black men's flesh
fall under the unflinching
gaze of overseer flint.

Bodies and bolts!
Sinewy bodies of black men
hammer steel bolts
while white officer flint looks on.

Glitter of gold!
Glistening black bodies
doused in sweat in the noonday sun
swirl satiation through overseer flint.
He looks on contented as black bodies
sweat in the noonday sun.

Glistening black bodies
toiling in the noonday sun
raise visions of gold before overseer flint.
Taunting tongues of gold caress
the mind of overseer flint.

After a hard day spent in shade
overseeing black
bodies glistening with sweat,
white officer flint dreams of molten
gold on glistening black bodies.

Birthright

In life we are conscientiously
schooled in self-negation.
So willingly we relinquish
our birthright, forgetting
in the interest of self-preservation.

Graduates in the mythology of dispossession
we lose our wariness of Trojan Horses.

In the days of yore, the trashy
trinkets of the West—nothing
more than broken glass pieces
garnished over to sparkle and titillate
the senses of those untutored
in the wiles of bondage—were
used to woe our forebears.

In the grip of wonderment
at such marvels, our wealth
was carted off in human
and natural resources.
The story doesn't change any.
Only the wiles of enslavement
do change.

Troy may no longer be around
but it pays to be wary of Trojan Horses

Eagles That Soar

We who are earthbound,
mere groundlings
incapable of self-elevation,
invent mechanical eagles
with high-powered wings
to satisfy our craving for a high.

We soar on mechanized wings
singing nearer my god to thee.
But today the eagle failed to soar,
its wings clipped by mechanical failure.

So we stand earthbound,
painfully aware of being
mere groundlings incapable
of raising ourselves off our feet
without mechanized help.

Grudgingly, we confess.
We miss so much the elevation
of spirit that rising even
on mechanical wings affords
us earthlings.

Ancestral Bonds

Taking Our Queue

If only I could undo four hundred
years of degradation, I would.
But I cannot traverse a chasm that deeply
entrenched in time
alone.

Can I choose to stand at the river bank
weeping into the river over the shards
of the broken water pot?
In the distance the bawling of the baby
forces action. The nursing mother is waiting
at home impatient for a drink of water.
Without the cooling drink, her breast
will not fill full. Her milk will not
be plentiful to quell the screams
of her impetuous baby.

Rather than spend the rest of our
productive days apologizing for crimes
committed against us with impunity,
or tear out our hair in lamentation
for implicating crimes by virtue
of our birthright, I am daring you
to take this hand of sisterhood,
of kinship, extended to you.

After all, you and I, we are co-losers in this game
of flesh-peddling, of profit and of loss.
Separated now by continents, labelled
and relabelled at the convenience of our betrayers,
we are the only true losers in this game
of skewed global commerce.
Hyenas feed off our carcasses.
They reap dividents on our degraded
flesh, while pronouncing moral judgment
against us, the victims.

Traumatized by the pain of severance,
you seem to have forgotten that when

you were wrenched from my life, I lost
my mother, father, grandparent, sister, brother,
neighbor, lover, bethrothed, playmate.
Soulmate, my blood, my kin, severed
from me without my consent.
Out of no choice I was forced to grow up
deprived of your warmth, of your laughter
which used to reverbarate in my heart
with the throb of atumpan drums.

Hyenas among us commit heinous acts.
We cannot tie a blood knot with any of them,
infested as their blood is with the bug of greed.
We have wasted too much time already
hurling accusations at each other over who
has betrayed whom—we the only real losers
in this game of devalued human flesh.

Taking our queue from immovable
foremothers, let us resolve never again
to wring our wrists in futility over
dropping the earthenware pot of palm soup.
The fufu is already pounded, ready
to be eaten.
Can't we fetch another pot, even if
it means settling for a metal one this time,
and making the soup over?
It may be nothing like the tenderly
tended palm soup our mothers had
waiting ready for us to eat.
Aromatic concoctions penetrating
the stupor of our alienation.
But even the ghost of a soup
salvaged by you and me from what
we can scoop up from mother's wasted
palm soup will be soup. It will be a good
enough accompaniment for mother's fufu
which is still waiting to kill our hunger pangs.

I refuse to quibble until the chickens
come home to roost about how we can

drop the earthenware-pot-of-palm-soup
when the fufu our mothers pounded
is still good, waiting, ready to be eaten.

Heritage

The streets of Accra.
The streets of Miami.
Old *Asafo* dance troupes.
Newly emerged rap groups.
Jitterbug. Cabbage patch.
Kpanlogo. Bambaya. Agbadza.
The sum of our shared heritage.

Traumas of the Middle Passage.
Forages of a greedy world.
Four hundred years of separation.
Rape. Pillage. Subjugation.
All these turn to ashes.
Unfazed, we form eternal kinships.
Forged by our forayed bodies.

The timely anticipation
of unvoiced needs and desires.
The absolute syncopation
of our ritual dances.
And now the living testimonials
to our kinship of bodies.
They, our shared heritage.

Seeding
(A cheer for cultivators of minds and knickknacks)

A seed
caringly dropped into nurtured soil,
with time sprouts into a giant *odum* tree.

A mind
caringly attended and schooled into becoming,
discerning grows.

Like the *odum* tree,
a mind nourished perennially bears fruit
to nourish generations.

Odum,
your branches tower for all to see
and wonder at your greatness.

Odum,
there is no death for you;
only life eternal, as you people the forest.

Odum,
like *asanteman* of old,
when a thousand are felled, another thousand spring up.

Odum,
you spring up houses to shelter minds
who spin words of wisdom to fuel other minds.

Ancestral Bonds

i
Handpicked for seduction
　　　into a sorority
　　　　　　of pseudo-universaldom,
　　　　　　　　　our brains are picked clean.

Submitted to a lobotomy
　　　that scrapes the imprint
　　　　　　of our cultural identity,
　　　　　　　　　we are carved a universal image.

ii
Believed purged
　　　of the culture specific,
　　　　　　we are proffered the robe—
　　　　　　　　　Insignia of Universalhood.

We don the robe
　　　amid effusive congratulations.
　　　　　　We become inducted
　　　　　　　　　into the Dome of Universaldom.

Catechized to shun
　　　ethnic configurations,
　　　　　　we are commended on escaping
　　　　　　　　　the confining claims to be
　　　　　　　　　　　　Akan
　　　　　　　　　　Hausa
　　　　　　　　　Mende
　　　　　　　Yoruba
　　　　Gikuyu
　　Luo

iii
But then one day,
　　　reality hits hard—
　　　　　　an awakening slap
　　　　　　　　　in the face of universalism.

WHO IS THERE TO CLAIM US BUT OUR OWN?

The blood of ancestors
      binds us in birth throes.
           Solidly, we are rooted
                 in ancestral selves.

Menua
(for Morisseau Leroy)

You are my sister,
Menua.
My blood sister.
We are children from one womb.

And you are my brother.
Menaba.
My blood brother
descended from a common womb.

We were birthed by the same woman,
Menua.
Long ago, before the season of marauders
forced us to walk divergent paths.

Our destinies are entwined,
Menaba.
Even though our paths have diverged,
our umbilical cords are buried in the same
homestead, fertilizing the same life crops.

My mother's children,
Menamba.
My life's quest has been to seek you out.
You, my stolen sisters and brothers.
I promised Adoma on her deathbed
I will not rest until I have found you.

You know, *Menuanom.*
The wishes of the dying are our testament.
So my *okra* will find no rest
until I have fulfilled my *nkrabea.*
The dead never leave us
even when they turn over.
Their spirits surround us in new
faces emerging from new wombs.

Menamba,

The spirit of Sunkwa
directed my path onto this route.
Menuanum,
Mensima's spirit led me to this lair
where her stolen children are secreted.
Menua,
The moment you looked into my face,
Nyaneba's spirit lighted out from your
eyes and reclaimed my spirit.

Goose pimples on the flesh
always betrays the condition of the spirit.
Before I could open my mouth to tell you
Adoma wants you to know she never forgot you,
you had seen that message in my eyes.
Before I could assure you Kwasima
knew in her womb you would return,
you already had gleaned that message
of our common destiny.

So as the *fontomfrom* sounds
and all of us fall in step to its beat,
the whole world stares, marveling
at our dance—our long inherited rhythm
freely flowing from our common step.

Stability

What do we crave the most in life?
Smooth transitions,
be they of seasons or political change.

So on this eve of change
to old/new political power,
we do beseech a smooth transition.

After ravaging storms, stillness sways.
Following devastating hurricanes,
silence lulls.

So having weathered
the ravages of political turmoil,
dare we not envision stability?

Here for Real
(for friends and family who need remembering)

Here today.
Gone tomorrow.
Isn't that the fate of all living things?

Yet, between now and the morrow,
we take our fate in hand
and we turn it around.

Proliferating ourselves in endless hugs,
we leave pieces of ourselves
clinging onto every touch.

The children we bear,
bear children to bear our names
and perpetuate us in memory's vault.

Something we say;
Something we do;
The special way we do our do.

The way we sashay
whenever we walk;
The way we roll our eyes in talk.

Our laughter ringing in another's ear.
The special cheer
our presence brings.

The stories we narrate;
The fashions we create;
The passion we generate in heated intimacy.

The whole while we journey,
tap-tapping through bottomless days,
we spread visible smears all over time's belly-button.

So today we're here, and tomorrow we're gone.
But how can we be gone-gone
when the world knows we've been here for real?